Prayers That Avail Much®
for Women

James 5:16

by
Germaine Copeland

And this is the confidence that we have in him, that,
if we ask any thing according to his will, he heareth
us: and if we know that he hear us, whatsoever we
ask, we know that we have the petitions that we
desired of him.

1 John 5:14,15

Harrison House

19 20 21   5 4 3

Prayers That Avail Much® for Women
Pocket Edition
ISBN 13: 978-1-57794-642-7
ISBN 10: 1-57794-642-1
Copyright © 2004 by Germaine Copeland
38 Sloan St.
Roswell, GA 30075

Published by Harrison House, Inc.
Shippensburg, PA 17257

Contents

Introduction

The prayers in this book will help you tap into the power of God for every area of your life — both at home and in the workplace. We receive many calls in our office from women of faith who are grappling with a culture that no longer values Christian principles. It is imperative that every believer has an active prayer to success-fully stand against the wiles of the devil.

Prayers That Avail Much for Women is a compilation of prayers that I believe will be helpful in scheduling and keeping your prayer appointments with God. These prayers will inspire and motivate you to spiritual growth and emotional wholeness.

Developing an effectual prayer life and consis-tently reading the Bible will bring you into a deeper and more intimate relationship with Father God. You learn to recognize and under-stand His nature, and appreciate the value He has placed on you.

You are God's woman, a new and different person with a fresh newness in all you do and think (Rom. 12:1,2 LB). The God Who created woman is the Lord Who gives the Word [of power]. He calls women to bear and publish the good news, and we are a great host (Ps. 68:11 AMP).

Ever learning, growing, and achieving, you are becoming a reflection of God's glory — a demonstration of Light and Love — in a culture that often appears to be anything but Christian.

My prayer is that you will find strength, comfort, courage, and fortitude as you pray *Prayers That Avail Much*®.

—Germaine Copeland, President
Word Ministries, Inc.

Personal Confessions

Jesus is Lord over my spirit, my soul, and my body (Phil. 2:9-11).

Jesus has been made unto me wisdom, righteousness, sanctification, and redemption. I can do all things through Christ Who strengthens me (1 Cor. 1:30; Phil. 4:13).

The Lord is my shepherd. I do not want. My God supplies all my need according to His riches in glory in Christ Jesus (Ps. 23; Phil. 4:19).

I do not fret or have anxiety about anything. I do not have a care (Phil. 4:6; 1 Pet. 5:6,7).

I am the Body of Christ. I am redeemed from the curse, because Jesus bore my sicknesses and carried my diseases in His own body. By His stripes I am healed. I forbid any sickness or disease to operate in my body. Every organ, every tissue, of my body functions in the perfection in which God created it to function. I honor God and bring glory to Him in my body (Gal. 3:13; Matt. 8:17; 1 Pet. 2:24; 1 Cor. 6:20).

I have the mind of Christ and hold the thoughts, feelings, and purposes of His heart (1 Cor. 2:16).

I am a believer and not a doubter. I hold fast to my confession of faith. I decide to walk by faith and practice faith. My faith comes by hearing and hearing by the Word of God. Jesus is the author and the developer of my faith (Heb. 4:14; Heb. 11:6; Rom. 10:17; Heb. 12:2).

The love of God has been shed abroad in my heart by the Holy Spirit, and His love abides in me richly. I keep myself in the Kingdom of light, in love, in the Word; and the wicked one touches me not (Rom. 5:5; 1 John 4:16; 1 John 5:18).

I tread upon serpents and scorpions and over all the power of the enemy. I take my shield of faith and quench his every fiery dart. Greater is He Who is in me than he who is in the world (Ps. 91:13; Eph. 6:16; 1 John 4:4).

I am delivered from this present evil world. I am seated with Christ in heavenly places. I reside in the Kingdom of God's dear Son. The law of the Spirit of life in Christ Jesus has made me free from the law of sin and death (Gal. 1:4; Eph. 2:6; Col. 1:13; Rom. 8:2).

I fear not, for God has given me a spirit of power, of love, and of a sound mind. God is on my side (2 Tim. 1:7; Rom. 8:31).

I hear the voice of the Good Shepherd. I hear my Father's voice, and the voice of a stranger I will not follow. I roll my works upon the Lord. I commit and trust them wholly to Him. He will cause my thoughts to become agreeable to His will, and so shall my plans be established and succeed (John 10:27; Prov. 16:3).

I am a world overcomer because I am born of God. I represent the Father and Jesus well. I am a useful member in the Body of Christ. I am His workmanship re-created in Christ Jesus. My Father God is all the while effectually at work in me both to will and do His good pleasure (1 John 5:4,5; Eph. 2:10; Phil. 2:13).

I let the Word dwell in me richly. He Who began a good work in me will continue until the day of Christ (Col. 3:16; Phil. 1:6).

1

To Walk in the Word

Father, in the name of Jesus, I commit myself to walk in the Word. Your Word living in me produces Your life in this world. I recognize that Your Word is integrity itself — steadfast, sure, eternal — and I trust my life to its provisions.

You have sent Your Word forth into my heart. I let it dwell in me richly in all wisdom. I meditate in it day and night so that I may diligently act on it. The Incorruptible Seed, the Living Word, the Word of Truth, is abiding in my spirit. That Seed is growing mightily in me now, producing Your nature, Your life. It is my counsel, my shield, my buckler, my powerful weapon in battle. The Word is a lamp to my feet and a light to my path. It makes my way plain before me. I do not stumble, for my steps are ordered in the Word.

The Holy Spirit leads and guides me into all the truth. He gives me understanding, discernment, and comprehension so that I am preserved from the snares of the evil one.

I delight myself in You and Your Word. Because of that, You put Your desires within my heart. I commit my way unto You, and You bring it to pass. I am confident that You are at work in me now both to will and to do all Your good pleasure.

I exalt Your Word, hold it in high esteem, and give it first place. I make my schedule around Your Word. I make the Word the final authority to settle all questions that confront me. I choose to agree with the Word of God, and I choose to disagree with any thoughts, conditions, or circumstances contrary to Your Word. I boldly and confidently say that my heart is fixed and established on the solid foundation — the living Word of God!

Scripture References

Psalms 37:4,5,23; 91:4; 112:7,8; 119:105

John 16:13

Hebrews 4:12

Ephesians 6:10

Colossians 1:9; 3:16; 4:2

Luke 18:1

Joshua 1:8

Philippians 2:13

1 Peter 1:23; 3:12

2 Corinthians 10:5

2

To Glorify God

Father, in view of Your mercy, I offer my body as a living sacrifice, holy and pleasing to You — this is my spiritual act of worship. It is [not in my own strength], for You, Lord, are all the while effectually at work in me — energizing and creating in me the power and desire — both to will and work for Your good pleasure.

Father, I will not draw back in fear, for then Your soul would have no pleasure in me. I was bought for a price, made Your very own. So, then, I honor You and bring glory to You in my body.

When I called on You in the day of trouble, You delivered me; I honor and glorify You. Thank You for delivering me and drawing me to Yourself out of the control and dominion of darkness and transferring me into the Kingdom of Your dear Son. I confess and praise You, O Lord my God, with my whole (united) heart; and I glorify Your name for evermore.

As a bondservant of Jesus Christ, I receive and develop the talents You have given me, for I would have You say of me, "Well done, you upright (honorable, admirable) and faithful servant!" I purpose to use the gifts (faculties, talents, qualities) according to the grace You have given me. I let my light so shine before men that they may see my moral excellence, my praise-worthy, noble, and good deeds, and recognize and honor and praise and glorify You, my Father.

In Jesus' name, I allow my life to lovingly express truth in all things — speaking truly, dealing truly, living truly. Whatever I do — no matter what it is — in word or deed, I do everything in the name of the Lord Jesus and in [dependence upon] His Person. Whatever my task, I work at it heartily (from the soul), as [something done] for You and not for men. Father God, to You be all glory and honor and praise. Amen.

Scripture References (AMP)

Romans 12:1,6	Psalms 50:15; 86:12
Philippians 2:13	Colossians 1:13; 3:17,23
Hebrews 10:38b	Matthew 5:16; 25:21
1 Corinthians 6:20	Ephesians 4:15

3

Knowing God's Will

Father, I thank You that You are instructing
me in the way that I should go and that You are
guiding me with Your eye. In the name of Jesus,
I submit to Your will, Your plan, and Your
purpose for my life. I hear the voice of the
Good Shepherd, for I know You and follow
You. You lead me in the paths of righteousness
for Your name's sake.

Thank You, Father, that my path is growing
brighter and brighter until it reaches the full
light of day. As I follow You, Lord, I believe my
path is becoming clearer each day.

Thank You, Father, that Jesus was made unto
me wisdom. Confusion is not a part of my life. I
am not confused about Your will for my life. I
trust in You and lean not unto my own understanding. As I acknowledge You in all my ways,
You are directing my paths. I believe that as I

trust in You completely, You will show me the path of life.

———

Scripture References

Psalms 16:11; 23:3; 32:8   Ephesians 5:19

John 10:3,4   1 Corinthians 1:30; 14:33

Proverbs 3:5,6; 4:18

4

Godly Wisdom in the Affairs of Life

Father, You said if anyone lacks wisdom, let him ask of You, and it shall be given him. Therefore, I ask in faith to be filled with the knowledge of Your will in all wisdom and spiritual understanding. I incline my ear unto wisdom, and apply my heart to understanding.

In the name of Jesus, I receive skill, godly wisdom, and instruction. I discern and comprehend the words of understanding and insight. As a person of understanding, I acquire skill and attain to sound counsels [so that I may be able to steer my course rightly].

Wisdom guards my life. I love, exalt, and prize her highly; she will bring me to honor because I embrace her. She gives to my head a wreath of gracefulness, a crown of beauty and glory. Length of days is in her right hand, and in her left hand are riches and honor.

Jesus has been made unto me wisdom, and in Him are all the treasures of [divine] wisdom and [all the riches of spiritual] knowledge and enlightenment. God has hidden away sound and godly wisdom and stored it up for me, for I am the righteousness of God in Christ Jesus.

Therefore, I will walk in paths of uprightness. When I walk, my steps shall not be hampered — my path will be clear and open; and when I run I shall not stumble. I take fast hold of instruction, and do not let her go; I guard her, for she is my life. I let my eyes look right on [with fixed purpose], and my gaze is straight before me. I consider well the path of my feet, and I let all my ways be established and ordered aright.

Father, in the name of Jesus, I look carefully to how I walk! I live purposefully and worthily and accurately, not as unwise and witless, but as a wise, sensible, intelligent person. I make the very most of my time — buying up every opportunity.

Scripture References

James 1:5,6a	1 Corinthians 1:30
Colossians 1:9b	Colossians 2:3 AMP
2 Corinthians 5:21	Ephesians 5:15,16 AMP
Proverbs 1:2-5; 2:2,7; 3:16; 4:6,8,9,11-13,25,26 AMP	

5

To Watch What You Say

Father, today I make a commitment to You, in the name of Jesus, to turn from idle words and foolishly speaking things that are contrary to my true desire. A word out of my mouth may seem of no account, but it can accomplish nearly anything — or destroy it!

In the name of Jesus, I submit to godly wisdom, which helps me control my tongue. I am determined that hell will not set my tongue on fire. Father, I renounce, reject, and repent of every word that has ever proceeded out of my mouth against You and Your Kingdom. I cancel its power and dedicate my mouth to speak excellent things. I shall speak the truth in love.

Because I am the righteousness of God in Christ Jesus, I set the course of my life for obedience, abundance, wisdom, health, joy. Set a guard over my mouth, O Lord; keep watch over the door of my lips. I purpose to guard my mouth and my tongue that I might keep myself from calamity.

Father, Your words are top priority to me. They are spirit and life. I let the Word dwell in me richly in all wisdom. The ability of God is released within me by the words that I speak and by the Word of God that I believe in my heart. Your words are living in me and at work in me. So I boldly say that I am speaking words of faith, power, love, and words of life. They are producing good things in my life and in the lives of others, in Jesus' name.

Scripture References

Ephesians 4:27; 5:4   2 Corinthians 5:21

2 Timothy 2:16   John 6:63

James 1:6; 3:5   Colossians 3:16

Proverbs 4:23; 8:6,7; 21:23 Philemon 6

6

To Live Free From Worry

Father, I thank You that I have been delivered from the power of darkness and translated into the Kingdom of Your dear Son. I commit to live free from worry, in the name of Jesus, for the law of the Spirit of life in Christ Jesus has made me free from the law of sin and death.

I humble myself under Your mighty hand that in due time You may exalt me. I cast the whole of my cares (name them) — all my anxieties, all my worries, all my concerns, once and for all — on You. You care for me affectionately and care about me watchfully. You sustain me. You will never allow the consistently righteous to be moved — made to slip, fall, or fail!

Father, I delight myself in You, and You perfect that which concerns me. I cast down imaginations (reasonings) and every high thing that exalts itself against the knowledge of You, and bring into captivity every thought to the obedience of Christ. I lay aside every weight and the sin of worry, which does try so easily to beset me. I run with patience the race that is set before me, looking unto Jesus, the Author and Finisher of my faith.

I thank You, Father, that You are able to keep that which I have committed unto You. I think on (fix my mind on) those things that are true, honest, just, pure, lovely, of good report, virtuous, and deserving of praise. I will not let my heart be troubled. I abide in Your Word, and Your Word abides in me. Therefore, Father, I do not forget what manner of person I am. I look into the perfect law of liberty and continue therein, being not a forgetful hearer, but a doer of the Word and thus blessed in my doing!

Thank You, Father. I am carefree. I walk in that peace which passes all understanding, in Jesus' name!

Scripture References

Colossians 1:13	Hebrews 12:1,2
Romans 8:2	2 Timothy 1:12
1 Peter 5:6,7 AMP	Philippians 4:6,8
Psalms 37:4,5; 55:22; 138:8	John 14:1; 15:7
2 Corinthians 10:5	James 1:22-25

7

Healing From Abuse

Lord, You are my High Priest, and I ask You to loose me from this "infirmity." The abuse I suffered pronounced me guilty and condemned. I was bound — in an emotional prison — crippled, and could in no wise lift up myself. You have called me to Yourself, and I have come.

Thank You for the anointing that binds up and heals the brokenness and emotional wounds of the past. Jesus, You are the Truth that makes me free.

Thank You for guiding me through the steps to emotional wholeness. You have begun a good work in me, and You will perform it until the day of Christ Jesus.

Father, I desire to live according to the Spirit of life in Christ Jesus. This Spirit of life in Christ, like a strong wind, has magnificently cleared the air, freeing me from a fated lifetime of brutal tyranny at the hands of abuse.

Since I am now free, it is my desire to forget those things that lie behind and strain forward to what lies ahead. I press on toward the goal to win the [supreme and heavenly] prize to which You in Christ Jesus are calling me upward. The past will no longer control my thinking patterns or my behavior.

Praise be to You! I am a new creature in Christ Jesus. Old things have passed away; and, behold, all things have become new. I declare and decree that henceforth I will walk in newness of life.

Father, I repent and renounce self-hatred and self-condemnation. I am Your child. You sent Jesus that I might have life and have it more abundantly. Thank You for the blood of Jesus that makes me whole.

It is my desire to throw all spoiled virtue and cancerous evil into the garbage. My Lord, You are the Gardener of my soul. In simple humility, I ask You to landscape me with the Word, making a salvation-garden of my life.

Father, by Your grace, I forgive my abuser(s) and ask You to bring him/her/them to repentance.

In the name of Jesus I pray. Amen.

_____

Scripture References

Luke 13:11,12

John 8:32; 10:10; 14:6

Philippians 1:6 KJV;
  3:13,14 AMP

Romans 6:4 KJV; 8:2 MESSAGE

2 Corinthians 5:17

1 John 1:7; 3:1,2

James 1:21 MESSAGE

Matthew 5:44

2 Peter 3:9

8

Letting Go of the Past

Father, I realize my helplessness in saving myself, and I glory in what Christ Jesus has done for me. I let go — put aside all past sources of my confidence — counting them worth less than nothing, in order that I may experience Christ and become one with Him.

Lord, I have received Your Son, and He has given me the authority (power, privilege, and right) to become Your child.

I unfold my past and put into proper perspective those things that are behind. I have been crucified with Christ, and I no longer live, but Christ lives in me. The life I live in the body, I live by faith in the Son of God, Who loved me and gave Himself for me. I trust in You, Lord, with all my heart; and I lean not on my own understanding. In all my ways I acknowledge You, and You will make my paths straight.

I want to know Christ and the power of His
resurrection and the fellowship of sharing in His
sufferings, becoming like Him in His death, and
so, somehow, to attain to the resurrection from
the dead. So, whatever it takes, I will be one
who lives in the fresh newness of life of those
who are alive from the dead.

I don't mean to say that I am perfect. I haven't
learned all I should even yet, but I keep working
toward that day when I will finally be all that
Christ saved me for and wants me to be.

I am bringing all my energies to bear on this
one thing: Regardless of my past, I look forward
to what lies ahead. I strain to reach the end of
the race and receive the prize for which You are
calling me up to heaven because of what Christ
Jesus did for me. In His name I pray. Amen.

Scripture References

Philippians 3:7-9,12-14 TLB   Galatians 2:20 NIV

Philippians 3:10,11 NIV   Proverbs 3:5,6 NIV

Philippians 3:13   John 1:12 AMP

Psalm 32:5 AMP   Romans 6:4

9

Strength To Overcome Cares and Burdens

Why are you cast down, O my inner self? And why should you moan over me and be disquieted within me?

Father, You set Yourself against the proud and haughty, but give grace [continually] unto the humble. I submit myself therefore to You, my God. In the name of Jesus, I resist the devil, and he flees from me. Jesus, I come to You, for I am heavy laden and overburdened. You cause me to rest — You ease, relieve, and refresh my soul. I take Your yoke upon me, and I learn of You for You are gentle (meek) and humble (lowly) in heart. Thank You for giving me rest — relief, ease, refreshment, recreation, and blessed quiet — for my soul. For Your yoke is wholesome (easy) — not harsh, hard, sharp, or pressing, but comfortable, gracious, and pleasant. Your burden is light and easy to be borne.

I cast my burden on You, Lord, [releasing the weight of it] and You sustain me; I thank You that You will never allow me to be moved — made to slip, fall, or fail.

In the name of Jesus, I withstand the devil. I am firm in my faith [against his onset] — rooted, established, strong, immovable, and determined. I cease from [the weariness and pain] of human labor. In the name of Jesus I am zealous, exerting myself and striving diligently to enter into the rest [of God] — to know and experience it for myself.

Father, I thank You that Your presence goes with me, and that You give me rest. I am still resting in You, Lord; I wait for You and patiently stay myself upon You. I am no longer fretting myself, nor allowing my heart to be troubled, neither shall I let it be afraid. I hope in You, my God, and wait expectantly for You; for I shall yet praise You, for You are the help of my countenance, and my God.

Scripture References (AMP)

Psalms 37:7; 42:11;
   55:22; 127:1a
James 4:6,7
Matthew 11:28-30

1 Peter 5:9a
Hebrews 4:10b,11
Exodus 33:14
John 14:27b

10

Healing for Damaged Emotions

Father, in the name of Jesus, I come to You with a feeling of shame and emotional hurt. I confess my transgressions to You [continually unfolding the past till all is told]. You are faithful and just to forgive me and cleanse me of all unrighteousness. You are my hiding place; You preserve me from trouble. You surround me with songs and shouts of deliverance. You saw me while I was being formed in my mother's womb; I am wonderfully made. I am Your handiwork, re-created in Christ Jesus.

Father, You have delivered me from the spirit of fear. I shall not be ashamed, confounded, or depressed. You gave me beauty for ashes, the oil of joy for mourning, the garment of praise for the spirit of heaviness, that I might be a tree of righteousness, the planting of the Lord, that You might be glorified. I speak in psalms, hymns, and spiritual songs, offering praise with my voice and making melody with my heart. Just as David did, I encourage myself in the Lord.

Father, thank You for Jesus. He was betrayed and crucified because of my misdeeds and raised to secure my acquittal, absolving me from all guilt before You. Father, You anointed Jesus and sent Him to bind up and heal my broken heart. You liberated me from the shame of my youth and the imperfections of my caretakers. In the name of Jesus I choose to forgive all who have wronged me in any way. Father, You have never left me without support. I am comforted and encouraged and confidently say, "The Lord is my Helper; I will not be seized with alarm. What can man do to me?"

My spirit is the candle of the Lord searching all the innermost parts of my being, and the Holy Spirit leads me into all truth. The sufferings of this present life cannot be compared with the glory that is about to be revealed to, in, for, and on me! The chastisement needful to obtain my peace and well-being was upon Jesus, and with His stripes I was healed and made whole. As a joint-heir with Jesus, I have a joyful

and confident hope of eternal salvation, which
will never disappoint, delude, or shame me.
Father, thank You for Your love that has been
poured out in my heart through the Spirit,
Whom You gave to me.

Scripture References

Psalms 32:5-7 AMP; 139

1 John 1:9

Deuteronomy 30:19

Ephesians 2:10; 5:19

2 Timothy 1:7

Isaiah 53:5b; 54:4; 61:1,3

Romans 4:24,25;
5:3-5; 8:18

Mark 11:25

Hebrews 13:5,6

Proverbs 20:27

John 16:13

11

Victory in a Healthy Lifestyle

Father, I am Your child, and Jesus is Lord over my spirit, soul, and body. I praise You because I am fearfully and wonderfully made. Your works are wonderful; I know that full well.

Lord, thank You for declaring Your plans for me — plans to prosper me and not to harm me, plans to give me hope and a future. I choose to renew my mind to Your plans for a healthy lifestyle. You have abounded toward me in all prudence and wisdom. Therefore, I give thought to my steps. Teach me knowledge and good judgment.

My body is for the Lord. So here is what I want to do with Your help, Father God. I choose to take my everyday, ordinary life — my sleeping, eating, going-to-work, and walking-around life — and place it before You as an offering. Embracing what You do for me is the best thing I can do for You.

Christ the Messiah will be magnified and will receive glory and praise in this body of mine and will be boldly exalted in my person. Thank You, Father, in Jesus' name! Hallelujah! Amen.

Scripture References

Psalms 119:66; 139:14   Romans 12:1 MESSAGE

Jeremiah 29:11   Philippians 1:20 AMP

Proverbs 14:15

12

Victory Over Fear

Father, when I am afraid, I will put my confidence in You. Yes, I will trust Your promises. And since I trust You, what can mere man do to me?

You have not given me a spirit of timidity, but of power and love and discipline (sound judgment). Therefore, I am not ashamed of the testimony of my Lord. I have not received a spirit of slavery leading to fear again, but I have received a spirit of adoption as a son, by which I cry out, "Abba! Father!"

Jesus, You delivered me, who, through fear of death, had been living all my life as a slave to constant dread. I receive the gift You left to me — peace of mind and heart! And the peace You give isn't fragile like the peace the world gives. I cast away troubled thoughts, and I choose not to be afraid. I believe in God; I believe also in You.

Lord, You are my Light and my Salvation; You protect me from danger — whom shall I fear? When evil men come to destroy me, they will stumble and fall! Yes, though a mighty army marches against me, my heart shall know no fear! I am confident that You will save me.

Thank You, Holy Spirit, for bringing these things to my remembrance when I am tempted to be afraid. I will trust in my God. In the name of Jesus, I pray.

Scripture References

Psalms 27:1-3; 56:3-5 TLB

2 Timothy 1:7,8 NASB

Romans 8:15 NASB

Hebrews 2:15 TLB

John 14:1,17 TLB

13

Overcoming Discouragement

Lord, I have exhausted all my possibilities and have found that I am powerless to change my situation. I believe; help me overcome my unbelief. All things are possible with You. I humble myself before You, and You will lift me up.

Jesus, You are my great High Priest, Who has gone through the heavens, and I hold firmly to the faith I profess. You sympathize with my weaknesses because You were tempted in every way, just as I am — yet You were without sin. In Your name I approach the throne of grace with confidence, so that I may receive mercy and find grace to help in my time of need.

You are mighty to deliver. Because of Your mighty hand, You will drive out the forces that have set themselves up against me. You are the Lord, Yahweh, the Promise-Keeper, the Almighty One.

Father, I believe that You have heard my cries. I will live to see Your promises of deliverance fulfilled in my life. You have not forgotten one word of Your promise; You are a Covenant-Keeper. You are a Father to me. Thank You for delivering me from the past that held me in bondage, and translating me into the Kingdom of love, peace, joy, and righteousness. I will no longer settle for the pain of the past. Where sin abounds, grace much more abounds.

Father, what You have promised, I will possess, in the name of Jesus. I am willing to get back into the good fight of faith that I might run the race with patient endurance and persistence. I rebuke the spirit of fear, for I am established in righteousness. Oppression and destruction shall not come near me. Whoever stirs up strife against me shall fall and surrender. I am more than a conqueror through Him Who loves me. In Jesus' name I pray. Amen.

Scripture References

*(This prayer is based on Exodus 5:22-6:11
and includes other verses where applicable.)*

Mark 9:24 NIV

Luke 18:27

1 Peter 5:6 NIV

Hebrews 4:14-16 NIV;
    12:1 AMP

Exodus 6:3,4 AMP

Genesis 49:22-26 AMP

1 Kings 8:56

Deuteronomy 26:8

Colossians 1:13

Romans 5:20; 8:37

1 Timothy 6:12

Isaiah 54:14-16

14

Overcoming Intimidation

Father, I come to You in the name of Jesus, confessing that intimidation has caused me to stumble. I ask Your forgiveness for thinking of myself as inferior, for I am created in Your image, and I am Your workmanship. Jesus said that the Kingdom of God is in me. Therefore, the power that raised Jesus from the dead dwells in me and causes me to face life with hope and divine energy.

The Lord is my Light and my Salvation; whom shall I fear? The Lord is the strength of my life; of whom shall I be afraid? Lord, You said that You would never leave me or forsake me. Therefore, I can say without any doubt or fear that You are my Helper, and I am not afraid of anything that mere man can do to me. Greater is He Who is in me than he who is in the world. If God is for me, who can be against me? I am free from the fear of man and public opinion.

Father, You have not given me a spirit of timidity — of cowardice, of craven and cringing and fawning fear — but You have given me a spirit of power and of love and of a calm and well-balanced mind and discipline and self-control. I can do all things through Christ, Who gives me the strength. Amen.

Scripture References

1 John 1:9; 4:4	2 Timothy 1:7
Luke 17:21	Ephesians 1:19,20; 2:10
Colossians 1:29	Psalm 1:27
Hebrews 13:5	Proverbs 29:25
Romans 3:31	Philippians 4:13

15

Overcoming a Sense of Hopelessness

Father, I come boldly before Your throne of grace asking for Your mercy and grace to help me in this time of need.

O God, You are the Hope of my Salvation. I ask You to listen to my prayer, and hide not Yourself from my supplication!

I am calling upon You, my God, to rescue me. You redeem my life in peace from the battle of hopelessness that is against me. I cast my burden on You, Lord, [releasing the weight of it] and You sustain me; You will never allow the [consistently] righteous to be moved (made to slip, fall, or fail).

When I feel afraid, I will choose to have confidence in and put my trust and reliance in You. By [Your help], God, I praise Your Word. By faith I proclaim and embrace Your uncondi-

tional love, and I will not fear. If God be for me
who can be against me?

You know my every sleepless night. Each tear
and heartache is answered with Your promise. I
am thanking You with all my heart. You pulled
me from the brink of death, my feet from the
cliff-edge of doom.

[What would have become of me], Lord, had
I not believed that I would see Your goodness in
the land of the living! I wait and hope for and
expect You; I am brave and of good courage; my
heart is stout and enduring.

Father, I give You all my worries and cares, for
You are always thinking about me and watching
over everything that concerns me. I am well
balanced and careful — vigilant, watching out
for attacks from Satan, my great enemy. By Your
grace I am standing firm, trusting You, and I
ask You to strengthen other Christians who are
going through the same sufferings. You, God,
are full of kindness through Christ and will give
me Your eternal glory.

In the name of Jesus, I am an overcomer by the blood of the Lamb and by the word of my testimony. Amen.

Scripture References

Hebrews 4:16

Psalms 55:1; 56:5,8,13

  MESSAGE

1 Peter 5:7-9

  AMP, TLB

Revelation 12:11

Psalms 27:13,14; 55:1,5,16,18,22; 56:2,4 AMP

16

Letting Go of Bitterness

Father, life seems so unjust, so unfair. The pain of rejection is almost more than I can bear. My past relationships have ended in strife, anger, rejection, and separation. Lord, help me to let go of all bitterness, indignation, wrath (passion, rage, bad temper), and resentment (anger, animosity).

You are the One Who binds up and heals the brokenhearted. I receive Your anointing that destroys every yoke of bondage. By faith I receive emotional healing, and thank You for giving me the grace to stand firm until the process is complete.

Thank You for wise counselors. I acknowledge the Holy Spirit as my wonderful Counselor. Thank You for helping me work out my salvation with fear and trembling. All the time You are working in me, giving me the desire and power to do what pleases you.

In the name of Jesus, I choose to forgive those who have wronged me. I purpose to live a life of forgiveness because You have forgiven me. With the help of the Holy Spirit, I get rid of all bitterness, rage, and anger, brawling, and slander, along with every form of malice. I desire to be kind and compassionate to others, forgiving them, just as in Christ You forgave me.

With the help of the Holy Spirit, I make every effort to live in peace with all men and to be holy, for I know that without holiness no one will see You, Lord. I purpose to see to it that I do not miss Your grace and that no bitter root grows up within me to cause trouble. I will watch and pray that I enter not into temptation or cause others to stumble.

Thank You, Father, for setting me free. Whom the Son has set free is free indeed! I declare that I have overcome resentment and bitterness by the blood of the Lamb and by the word of my testimony. In Jesus' name. Amen.

———

Scripture References

Ephesians 4:31 AMP;
  4:31,32 NIV
Luke 4:18
Isaiah 10:27
Proverbs 11:14
John 8:36 KJV;
  15:26 AMP

Philippians 2:12,13 NIV
Matthew 5:44; 26:41
Hebrews 12:14,15 NIV
Romans 14:21
Jeremiah 1:12 AMP
Revelation 12:11

17

Health and Healing

Father, in the name of Jesus, I come before You asking You to heal me. It is written that the prayer of faith will save the sick, and the Lord will raise him up. And if I have committed sins, I will be forgiven. I let go of all unforgiveness, resentment, anger, and bad feelings toward anyone.

My body is the temple of the Holy Spirit, and I desire to be in good health. I seek truth that will make me free — both spiritual and natural (good eating habits, medications if necessary, and appropriate rest and exercise). You bought me at a price, and I desire to glorify You in my spirit and my body — they both belong to You.

Thank You, Father, for sending Your Word to heal me and deliver me from all my destructions. Jesus, You are the Word Who became flesh and dwelt among us. You bore my griefs (pains) and carried my sorrows (sickness). You were pierced through for my transgressions and crushed for my iniquities; the chastening for my well-being fell upon You, and by Your scourging I am healed.

Father, I give attention to Your words and incline my ear to Your sayings. I will not let them depart from my sight, but I will keep them in the midst of my heart, for they are life and health to my whole body.

Since the Spirit of Him Who raised Jesus from the dead dwells in me, He Who raised Christ from the dead will also give life to my mortal body through His Spirit, Who dwells in me.

Thank You that I will prosper and be in health, even as my soul prospers. Amen.

Scripture References

James 5:15 NKJV

1 Corinthians 6:19,20

Psalms 103:3-5 NASB; 107:20

John 1:14

Isaiah 53:4,5 NASB

Proverbs 4:21,22 NASB

Romans 8:11 NKJV

3 John 2

18

Safety

Father, in the name of Jesus, I thank You for watching over Your Word to perform it. In the name of Jesus I dwell in the secret place of the Most High, and I shall remain stable and fixed under the shadow of the Almighty, Whose power no foe can withstand.

Father, You are my refuge and my fortress. No evil shall befall me — no accident shall overtake me — no plague or calamity shall come near my home. You give Your angels special charge over me, to accompany and defend and preserve me in all my ways of obedience and service. They are encamped around about my family.

Father, You are my confidence, firm and strong. You keep my foot from being caught in a trap or hidden danger. Thank You for keeping me safe and easing me day by day.

Traveling — As I go, I say, "Let me pass over to the other side," and I have what I say. I walk on my way securely and in confident trust, for my heart and mind are firmly fixed and stayed on You, and I am kept in perfect peace.

Sleeping — Father, I sing for joy upon my bed because You sustain me. In peace I lie down and sleep, for You alone, Lord, make me dwell in safety. I lie down, and I am not afraid. My sleep is sweet, for You give blessings to me in sleep. Thank You, Father, in Jesus' name. Amen.

Continue to feast and meditate upon all of Psalm 91 for yourself and your loved ones!

Scripture References

Psalms 3:5; 34:7; 112:7;   Jeremiah 1:12
  127:2; 149:5   Proverbs 3:23,24,26 AMP
Psalms 4:8;   Isaiah 26:3; 49:25
  91:1,2,10,11 AMP   Mark 4:35 AMP

19

Peaceful Sleep

Father, thank You for peaceful sleep, and Your angels that encamp around us who fear You. You deliver us and keep us safe. The angels excel in strength, do Your Word, and heed the voice of Your Word. You give Your angels charge over me, to keep me in all my ways.

I bring every thought, every imagination, and every dream into the captivity and obedience of Jesus Christ. Father, I thank You that even as I sleep my heart counsels me and reveals to me Your purpose and plan. Thank You for sweet sleep, for You promised Your beloved sweet sleep. Therefore, my heart is glad, and my spirit rejoices. My body and soul rest and confidently dwell in safety. Amen.

Scripture References

Psalms 16:7-9; 91:11;
   103:20; 127:2
2 Corinthians 10:5

Proverbs 3:24
Matthew 16:19; 18:18

20

Prosperity

Father, I come to You, in the name of Jesus, concerning my financial situation. You are a very present help in trouble, and You are more than enough. Your Word declares that You shall supply all my need according to Your riches in glory by Christ Jesus.

(If you have not been giving tithes and offerings, include this statement of repentance in your prayer.) Forgive me for robbing You in tithes and offerings. I repent and purpose to bring all my tithes into the storehouse that there may be food in Your house. Thank You for wise financial counselors and teachers who are teaching me the principles of good stewardship.

Lord of hosts, You said, "Try Me now in this, and I will open the windows of heaven and pour out for you such blessing that there will not be room enough to receive it." You will rebuke the devourer for my sake, and my heart is filled with thanksgiving.

Lord, my God, I shall remember that You are the One Who gives me the power to get wealth that You may establish Your covenant. In the name of Jesus, I worship You only, and I will have no others gods before me.

You are able to make all grace — every favor and earthly blessing — come to me in abundance, so that I am always, and in all circumstances, furnished in abundance for every good work and charitable donation. Amen.

Scripture References:

Psalm 56:1

Philippians 4:19

Malachi 3:8-12

Deuteronomy 8:18,19

2 Corinthians 9:8 AMP

21

Developing Healthy Friendships

Father, help me to meet new friends —
friends who will encourage me. May I find in
these friendships the companionship and
fellowship You have ordained for me. I know
that You are my source of love, companionship,
and friendship. Your love and friendship are
expressed through my relationship with You and
members of the Body of Christ.

According to Proverbs 27:17 CEV, iron
sharpens iron, so friends sharpen the minds of
each other. As we learn from each other, may
we find a worthy purpose in our relationship.
Keep me well-balanced in my friendships, so
that I will always please You rather than
pleasing other people.

I ask for divine connections — good friendships ordained by You. Thank You for the
courage and grace to let go of detrimental
friendships. I ask and receive, by faith, discern-

ment for developing healthy relationships. Your Word says that two are better than one, because if one falls, there will be someone to lift that person up.

Father, You know the hearts of people, so I won't be deceived by outward appearances. Bad friendships corrupt good morals. Thank You for quality friends who help me build a stronger character and draw me closer to You. Help me be a friend to others and to love my friends at all times. I will laugh with those who laugh, I will rejoice with those who rejoice, and I will weep with those who weep. Teach me what I need to know to be a quality friend.

Develop in me a fun personality and a good sense of humor. Help me to relax around people and to be myself — the person You created me to be. Instruct my heart and mold my character, that I may be faithful and trustworthy over the friendships You are sending into my life.

Father, Your Son Jesus is my best Friend. He is a Friend Who sticks closer than a brother. He defined the standard when He said in John 15:13, "Greater love hath no man than this, that a man lay down his life for his friends." Thank You, Lord, that I can entrust myself and my need for friends into Your keeping. I submit to the leadership of the Holy Spirit, in the name of Jesus. Amen.

Scripture References

Proverbs 13:20 NIV;
   17:17; 18:24

Ephesians 5:30 NIV

Philippians 2:2,3 NIV

Psalms 37:4,5; 84:11 NIV

Ecclesiastes 4:9,10 NIV

1 Corinthians 15:33 AMP

James 1:17 NIV

Romans 12:15

22

Finding Favor With Others

Father, in the name of Jesus, You make Your face to shine upon and enlighten _____ and are gracious (kind, merciful, and giving favor) to him/her. _____ is the head and not the tail. _____ is above only and not beneath.

Thank You for favor for _____, who seeks Your Kingdom and Your righteousness and diligently seeks good. _____ is a blessing to You, Lord, and is a blessing to *(name them: family, neighbors, business associates, etc.).* Grace (favor) is with _____, who loves the Lord Jesus in sincerity. _____ extends favor, honor, and love to *(names).* _____ is flowing in Your love, Father. You are pouring out upon _____ the spirit of favor. You crown him/her with glory and honor, for he/she is Your child — Your workmanship.

_____ is a success today. _____ is someone very special with You, Lord.

_____ is growing in the Lord — waxing strong in spirit. Father, You give _____ knowledge and skill in all learning and wisdom.

You bring _____ to find favor, compassion, and loving-kindness with _____ *(names)*. _____ obtains favor in the sight of all who look upon him/her this day, in the name of Jesus. _____ is filled with Your fullness — rooted and grounded in love. You are doing exceeding abundantly above all that _____ asks or thinks, for Your mighty power is taking over in _____.

Thank You, Father, that _____ is well-favored by You and by man, in Jesus' name!

Scripture References

Numbers 6:25	Zechariah 12:10
Deuteronomy 28:13	Psalm 8:5
Matthew 6:33	Luke 2:40
Proverbs 11:27	Daniel 1:9,17
Ephesians 2:10; 3:19,20; 6:24	Esther 2:15,17
Luke 6:38	

23

Finding a Mate

Father, I submit to the constant ministry of transformation by the Holy Spirit, making my petition known to You. Prepare me for marriage by bringing everything to light that has been hidden. I know in Whom I have placed my confidence, and that the work, whether I marry or not, is safe in Your hands until that Day.

I lay aside every weight and the sins which so easily ensnare me, and run with endurance the race that is set before me, looking unto Jesus, the Author and Finisher of my faith. I consider Him Who endured such hostility from sinners against Himself, lest I become weary and discouraged in my soul. He makes intercession for me.

I turn my back on the turbulent desires of youth and give my positive attention to goodness, integrity, love, and peace in company with all those who approach You in sincerity. Father, I desire and earnestly seek (aim at and strive after) first of all Your Kingdom and Your righteousness (Your way of doing and being right), and then all these things taken together will be given me besides. So I do not worry and will not be anxious about tomorrow.

I am persuaded that I can trust You because You first loved me. You chose me in Christ before the foundation of the world. In Him the whole fullness of Deity (the Godhead) continues to dwell in bodily form [giving complete expression of the divine nature], and in Him I am made full and have come to the fullness of life [in Christ].

I am filled with the Godhead — Father, Son, and Holy Spirit — and I reach toward full spiritual stature. And He (Christ) is the Head of all rule and authority [of every angelic principality and power]. So, because of Jesus, I am complete; Jesus is my Lord.

I come before You, Father, expressing my desire for a Christian mate. I petition that Your will be done in my life. Now I enter into that blessed rest by adhering to, trusting in, and relying on You. In Jesus' name. Amen.

Scripture References

Matthew 6:10 KJV;
  6:33,34 AMP
1 Corinthians 4:5
Hebrews 4:10 KJV;
  12:1-3 NKJV

2 Timothy 1:12 PHILLIPS
1 John 4:19
Colossians 2:9,10 AMP
John 14:1 AMP

24

Preparing Self for Marriage

Father, sometimes being single can be so lonely. Please comfort me in these times. Help me to remember to work on being whole and mature when You bring the right person into my life. Show me how to be responsible for myself and how to allow others to be responsible for themselves.

Teach me about boundaries, what they are and how to establish them instead of walls. Teach me about Your love and how to speak the truth in love, as Jesus did.

Father, I don't want to be a hindrance to my future spouse, to You, or to myself. Help me to take a good look at myself, at my self-image. Lead me to people — teachers, preachers, counselors — and to things — books, tapes, seminars — anyone and anything You can use to teach me Your ways of being and doing right and being whole.

Teach me how to choose the mate You would have for me. Give me the wisdom I need to see clearly, and not to be double-minded. Help me to recognize the qualities You would have me look for in a mate.

Father, thank You for revealing to me that the choice of a mate is not to be based only on emotions and feelings, but that You have very definite guidelines in the Bible for me to use. I know that when I put these principles into practice, I will save myself a lot of pain and trouble.

Thank You that You are not trying to make things hard for me, but that You know me better than I know myself. You know my situation — You know the beginning from the end. You know the qualities and attributes that are needed in another person that will make me happy in our shared life together and that person happy with me.

I pray that You will keep my foot from being caught in a hidden trap or danger. I cast the care of this decision on You, knowing that You will cause my thoughts to come in line with

Your will so that my plans will be established and succeed. In Jesus' name I pray, amen.

Scripture References

1 Corinthians 1:3,4 NIV   James 1:5-8
Ephesians 4:15   Proverbs 3:26; 16:3 AMP
Matthew 6:33 AMP

25

Wives

In the name of Jesus, I cultivate inner beauty, the gentle, gracious kind that God delights in. I choose to be a good, loyal wife to my husband and address him with respect. I will not be anxious and intimidated. I purpose to be, by God's grace, agreeable, sympathetic, loving, compassionate, and humble. I will be a blessing and also receive blessings.

By the grace of God, I yield to the constant ministry of transformation by the Holy Spirit. I am being transformed into a gracious woman who retains honor, and a virtuous woman who is a crown to my husband. I purpose to walk wisely that I may build my house. Houses and riches are the inheritance of fathers, and a prudent wife is from the Lord. In Christ I have redemption through His blood, the forgiveness of sins, according to the riches of His grace which He made to abound toward me in all wisdom and prudence.

Holy Spirit, I ask You to help me understand and support my husband in ways that show my support for Christ.* Teach me to function so that I preserve my own personality while responding to his desires. We are one flesh, and I realize that this unity of persons that preserves individuality is a mystery, but that is how it is when we are united to Christ. So I will keep on loving my husband and let the miracle keep happening!

Just as my husband gives me what is due me, I seek to be fair to my husband. I share my rights with my husband.

Strength and dignity are my clothing, and my position in my household is strong. My family is in readiness for the future. The bread of idleness (gossip, discontent, and self-pity) I will not eat. I choose to conduct the affairs of my household wisely, realizing that wisdom from above is pure, peaceable, gentle, willing to yield, full of mercy and good fruits, without partiality, and without hypocrisy. Amen.

Scripture References

Ephesians 1:7,8 NKJV;
  5:22-33* MESSAGE

Proverbs 11:16; 12:4;
  14:1; 19:14

Proverbs 31:25-27 AMP

Matthew 16:19 NKJV

1 Peter 3:1-5,8,9 MESSAGE

Psalm 51:10 NKJV

2 Corinthians 3:18

1 Corinthians 7:2-5
  PHILLIPS

James 3:17,18 NKJV

---

* The Message and Paraphrase The Heart of Paul, Ben
  Campbell Johnson, © 1976, A Great Love, Inc., Toccoa,
  GA 30577.

26

The Home

Father, I thank You for blessing us with all spiritual blessings in Christ Jesus.

Our house is built through skillful and godly wisdom, and established on a sound and good foundation by understanding. And by knowledge the chambers (of its every area) are filled with all precious and pleasant riches — great priceless treasure. Prosperity and welfare are in our house, in the name of Jesus.

Our house is founded on the Rock — revelation knowledge of Your Word, Father. Jesus is our Cornerstone, and the Lord of our household.

Whatever may be our tasks, we work at them heartily as something done for You, Lord, and not for men. We love each other with the God kind of love, and we dwell in peace. My home is deposited into Your charge, entrusted to Your protection and care.

Father, as for me and my house, we shall serve the Lord, in Jesus' name. Hallelujah! Amen.

Scripture References

Ephesians 1:3

Proverbs 12:7; 24:3,4 AMP

Proverbs 15:6

Psalm 112:3

Luke 6:48

Acts 4:11; 16:31; 20:32

Philippians 2:10,11

Colossians 3:14,15,23

Joshua 24:15

27

When Desiring To Have a Baby

Our Father, my spouse and I bow our knees
unto You. Father of our Lord Jesus Christ, of
whom the whole family in heaven and on earth
is named, we pray that You would grant to us,
according to the riches of Your glory, to be
strengthened with might by Your Spirit in the
inner man. Christ dwells in our hearts by faith,
that we — being rooted and grounded in love —
may be able to comprehend with all the saints
what is the breadth, and length, and depth, and
height of the love of Christ, which passes
knowledge, that we might be filled with all the
fullness of God.

Hallelujah! We praise You, O Lord, for You
give children to the childless wife, so that she
becomes a happy mother. And we thank You
that You are the One Who is building our
family. As Your children and inheritors through

Jesus Christ, we receive Your gift — the fruit of the womb, Your child, as our reward.

We praise You, our Father, in Jesus' name, for we know that whatsoever we ask, we receive of You, because we keep Your commandments and do those things which are pleasing in Your sight.

Thank You, Father, that we are a fruitful vine within our house; our children will be like olive shoots around our table. Thus shall we be blessed because we fear the Lord.

In Jesus' name we pray. Amen.

Scripture References

Ephesians 3:14-19   Psalm 127:3
Psalms 113:9; 128:3,4 AMP   1 John 3:22,23 AMP

28

Godly Order in Pregnancy and Childbirth

Father, in Jesus' name, I confess Your powerful Word this day over my pregnancy and the birth of my child. I put on the whole armor of God so that I may be able to stand against all the tricks and traps of the devil. I stand in faith during this pregnancy and birth, not giving any room to fear. I thank You and praise You for giving me a spirit of power, love, and a sound mind. May You be glorified in all things.

Heavenly Father, I confess that You are my refuge. I am thankful that You have put angels at watch over my unborn child and me. I cast all the care and burden of this pregnancy over on You. Your grace is sufficient for me through this pregnancy; You strengthen my weaknesses.

Father, Your Word declares that my unborn child was created in Your image, fearfully and wonder- fully made to praise You. You have made me a joyful mother, and I am blessed with a heritage from You as my reward. I commit this child to You and pray that he/she will grow and call me blessed.

I am not afraid of pregnancy or childbirth, because I trust You, Father. Thank You that all decisions regarding my pregnancy and delivery will be godly, that the Holy Spirit will intervene. I know that Jesus died on the cross to take away my sickness and pain. Having accepted Your Son Jesus as my Savior, I confess that my child will be born healthy and completely whole. Thank You, Father, for the law of the Spirit of life in Christ Jesus, which has made me and my child free from the law of sin and death!

Father, thank You for protecting me and my baby and for our good health. Amen.

Scripture References

Psalms 91:1,2,10,11; 112:7; 113:9; 127:3; 139:14
Jeremiah 1:12; 33:3
Isaiah 55:11
Hebrews 4:12
Ephesians 6:11,12,16
1 Peter 4:11; 5:7

2 Corinthians 12:9
Genesis 1:26
Proverbs 31:28
Matthew 8:17; 18:18
Romans 8:2
James 4:7
John 4:13

29

Beginning Each Day

Father, I come before You rejoicing, for this is the day which You have made and I will be glad in it. To obey is better than sacrifice, so I submit to Your will today that my plans and purposes may be conducted in a manner that brings honor and glory to You. Cause me to be spiritually and mentally alert in this time of meditation and prayer.

I place my family into Your keeping, knowing that You are able to keep that which I commit to You against that Day. Thank You for the angels that You have commanded concerning me and my family to guard us in all our ways; they will lift us up in their hands so that we will not strike our foot against a stone.

Thank You, Lord, for the tremendous success in our organization and for the increase in profits and productivity we have enjoyed. Thank You for continuing to influence every person and every decision in this business. Thank You for Your faithfulness to us day by day and for helping us to become all that You desire us to be.

Thank You, Father, for helping to make us a company that continues to grow and expand. We recognize that without Your help, it would not be possible; with it, we can prosper and have good success. I continue to thank You for the many blessings that You have poured out upon us.

I especially thank You for the co-laborers with whom I will be interacting today. Give me words of wisdom, words of grace, that I might encourage them and build them up. Father, I kneel before You, from Whom Your whole family in heaven and on earth derives its name. I pray that out of Your glorious riches You may strengthen each one with power through Your Spirit in his inner being, so that Christ may dwell in each heart through faith.

Now to Him Who is able to do immeasurably more than all we ask or imagine, according to His power that is at work within us, to Him be the glory in this company and in Christ Jesus throughout all generations, for ever and ever! In Jesus' name I pray. Amen.

Scripture References

Psalms 91:11,12 NIV;   Lamentations 3:22,23
    118:24   Joshua 1:8
1 Samuel 15:22   Ephesians 3:14-17,20 NIV
2 Timothy 1:12

30

Being Equipped for Success

Father, thank You that the entrance of Your words gives light. Your Word is alive and powerful. You have given me a spirit of power, love, and a calm and well-balanced mind and discipline and self-control. You have qualified me as a minister of a new covenant.

In Jesus' name, I walk out of the realm of failure into the arena of success, giving thanks to You for qualifying me to share the inheritance of the saints in the Light.

I praise You, Father, for giving me every blessing in heaven because I belong to Christ. You have given me all I need for life and godliness through my knowledge of Him Who called me by His own glory and goodness. I rejoice in Jesus, Who has given me abundant life. I am a new creation, for I am (engrafted) in Christ. The old has passed away. Behold, the fresh and new has come! I forget what is behind and reach forth unto those things which are before me. I am crucified with Christ: nevertheless I live; yet not I, but Christ lives in me: and I live by the faith of the Son of God, Who loved me and gave Himself for me.

Father, I attend, consent, and submit to Your sayings. I will keep them in the center of my heart. For they are life *(success)* to me, healing and health to all my flesh. I keep and guard my heart above all, for out of it flow the springs of life. I will not let mercy, kindness, and truth forsake me. I bind them about my neck; I write them upon the tablet of my heart. Therefore, I will find favor, good understanding, and high esteem in the sight of God and man.

Father, my delight and desire are in Your Law, and on it I habitually meditate (ponder and study) day and night. Therefore, I am like a tree firmly planted by the streams of water, ready to bring forth my fruit in my season; my leaf shall not wither, and everything I do shall prosper. *Now thanks be unto God, which always causeth us to triumph in Christ!*

Scripture References

2 Corinthians 2:14

2 Corinthians 3:5;
  5:17 AMP

Psalms 1:2,3 AMP;
  119:130

Proverbs 3:3,4;
  4:20-23 AMP

Hebrews 4:12 AMP

2 Timothy 1:7 AMP

Colossians 1:12,13 AMP

Ephesians 1:3 TLB

John 10:10 AMP

Philippians 3:13

Galatians 2:20

2 Peter 1:3 NIV

31

Assuring the Success of a Business

Father, I commit my works (the plans and cares of my business) to You, trusting them wholly to You. Since You are effectually at work in me [You cause my thoughts to become agreeable with Your will] so that my (business) plans shall be established and succeed.

In the name of Jesus, I submit to every kind of wisdom and understanding (practical insight and prudence) which You have lavished upon me in accordance with the riches and generosity of Your gracious favor.

Father, I obey Your Word by making an honest living with my own hands so that I may be able to give to those in need. In Your strength and according to Your grace, I provide for myself and my own family. Thank You for making all grace (every favor and earthly blessing) come to me in abundance, so that I, having all sufficiency in all things, may abound to every good work.

Father, thank You for the ministering spirits that You have assigned to go forth to minister on my behalf and bring in trade. In Jesus' name my light shall so shine before all men that they may see my good works and glorify You.

Thank You for the grace to remain diligent in seeking knowledge and skill in areas in which I am inexperienced. I ask You for wisdom and the ability to understand righteousness, justice, and fair dealing [in every area and relationship]. I affirm that I am faithful and committed to Your Word. My life and business are founded upon its principles.

Thank You, Father, for the success of my business! In Jesus' name I pray. Amen.

Scripture References

Proverbs 2:9; 4:20-22; 16:3; 22:29 AMP

Ephesians 1:7,8; 4:28 AMP   Matthew 5:14,16

Philippians 2:13 AMP   1 Timothy 5:8 AMP

Hebrews 1:14   2 Corinthians 9:8 AMP

32

Making a Difficult Decision

Father, I bring this decision before You. It is a difficult one for me to make in the natural, but I know that with You it can be an easy one.

I ask You, Lord, to help me see both sides of this issue and to consider all the facts involved in it. Help me to properly evaluate both the positive and negative attributes of this situation.

Lord, I recognize that an important part of being an excellent manager is decisiveness. As I process the information and consider the possible repercussions or benefits of this decision, help me to avoid the paralysis of analysis. Help me to get the information I need and to evaluate it carefully and wisely.

Help me, Father, to hear Your voice, and so to make the right and correct decision in this case. Keep me from acting in haste but also from delaying too long to reach a decision.

Father, help me not to be influenced by my own personal wants or desires concerning this matter under consideration. Instead, help me to perceive and choose what is best for my department or company, regardless of how I may feel about it personally. Help me to undertake and carry out this decision-making process accurately and objectively.

Thank You for Your guidance and direction in this situation. In Jesus' name I pray. Amen.

Scripture References

Isaiah 11:2 AMP

Colossians 4:1 NIV

Proverbs 28:1

John 10:27

Philippians 2:3 NIV

Judges 6:12

33

Prayer for an Increase in Personal Productivity

Father, I come to You out of frustration because I am not pleased with my performance on the job. It seems that I am not producing that which I should be producing because I am just not as efficient or effective as I need to be.

Lord, I ask for Your help in planning my day, paying attention to my duties, staying focused on my assignment, establishing priorities in my work, and making steady progress toward my objectives.

Give me insight, Father. Help me to see any habits that I may have that might tend to make me nonproductive. Reveal to me ways to better handle the tedious tasks I must perform so that I can achieve the greatest results possible. Help me to organize my efforts, schedule my activities, and budget my time.

From books, by Your Spirit, through the people who work with me, or by whatever means You choose, Lord, reveal to me that which I need to know and do in order to become a more productive, fruitful worker.

My heart's desire is to give my very best to You and to my employer. When I become frustrated because that is not taking place, help me, Father, by the power of Your Spirit to do whatever is necessary to correct that situation so that I can once again function with accuracy and proficiency.

Thank You, Lord, for bringing all these things to pass in my life.

In Jesus' name I pray. Amen.

Scripture References

Psalms 118:24 KJV; 119:99 AMP   1 Corinthians 4:5

Proverbs 9:10; 16:9; 19:21 AMP   Ephesians 1:17

34

Undertaking a New Project

Lord, I lift up to You this new project which we are considering. I feel that it is one we should be a part of, something we should do, but I seek Your wisdom concerning it.

If it is not of You, Lord, please put a check in our spirits. Direct us to stop planning and working on it and to put a halt to any further waste of time and energy.

If it is of You, Father, then I thank You for Your counsel and assistance concerning it. Give us understanding and discernment in the preparation stages as we gather the information we need to devise a course of action and to plan the budget for the work. Help us to accumulate the facts and figures we need to carry out this plan in accordance with Your will and purpose.

Thank You, Lord, for Your insight and wisdom. I ask You to give each of us guidance and direction by Your Holy Spirit so we will know how to assimilate the information we gather and use it to maximum advantage. Reveal to us any hidden costs or expenses so that we can take them into account in preparing an accurate budget and detailed forecast of both time and money.

Give all of us involved in this project the ability to concentrate our attention and focus our efforts so that we can successfully complete this undertaking and thereby bring honor and glory to You through it.

In Jesus' name I pray. Amen.

Scripture References

Proverbs 8:12 AMP

Isaiah 11:2 NIV

Jeremiah 29:11-13 KJV;
   33:3 NIV

Ephesians 1:8,9,17 AMP

Luke 12:2 NIV

Romans 12:2 NIV

35

American Government

Father, in Jesus' name, we give thanks for the United States and its government. We pray and intercede for the leaders in our land: the president, the representatives, the senators, the judges, the governors, the mayors, the police officers, and all those in authority over us in any way. We pray that the Spirit of the Lord rests upon them.

We believe that skillful and godly wisdom has entered into the heart of our president and knowledge is pleasant to him. Discretion watches over him; understanding keeps him and delivers him from evil.

Father, we ask that You encircle the president with people who make their hearts and ears attentive to godly counsel and do right in Your sight. We believe You cause them to be people of integrity who are obedient concerning us that we may lead a quiet and peaceable life in all godliness and honesty. We pray that the upright shall dwell in our government, that leaders blameless and complete in Your sight shall remain but the wicked shall be cut off.

Your Word declares that "blessed is the nation whose God is the Lord" (Ps. 33:12). We receive Your blessing. Father, You are our Refuge and Stronghold in times of trouble (high cost, destitution, and desperation). So we declare with our mouths that Your people dwell safely in this land, and we *prosper* abundantly. We are more than conquerors through Christ Jesus!

It is written in Your Word that the heart of the king is in the hand of the Lord, and You turn it whichever way You desire. We believe the heart of our leader is in Your hand and that his decisions are directed of the Lord.

We give thanks unto You that the good news of the Gospel is published in our land. The Word of the Lord prevails and grows mightily in the hearts and lives of the people. We give thanks for this land and the leaders You have given to us, in Jesus' name.

Jesus is Lord over the United States! Amen.

Scripture References

1 Timothy 2:1-3	Deuteronomy 28:10,11
Proverbs 2:10-12,21,22; 21:1	Romans 8:37 AMP
Psalms 9:9; 33:12	Acts 12:24

Prayer of Salvation

God loves you—no matter who you are, no matter what your past. God loves you so much that He gave His one and only begotten Son for you. The Bible tells us, "...whoever believes in him shall not perish but have eternal life" (John 3:16 NIV). Jesus laid down His life and rose again so that we could spend eternity with Him in heaven and experience His absolute best on earth. If you would like to receive Jesus into your life, say the following prayer out loud and mean it from your heart.

Heavenly Father, I come to You admitting that I am a sinner. Right now, I choose to turn away from sin, and I ask You to cleanse me of all unrighteousness. I believe that Your Son, Jesus, died on the cross to take away my sins. I also believe that He rose again from the dead so that I might be forgiven of my sins and made righteous through faith in Him. I call upon the name of Jesus Christ to be the Savior and Lord of my life. Jesus, I choose to follow You and ask that You fill me with the power of the Holy Spirit. I declare that right now I am a child of God. I am free from sin and full of the righteousness of God. I am saved in Jesus' name. Amen.

If you prayed this prayer to receive Jesus Christ as your Savior for the first time, please contact us on the Web at **www.harrisonhouse.com** to receive a free book.

Or you may write to us at

Harrison House
P.O. Box 35035
Tulsa, Oklahoma 74153

About the Author

Germaine Griffin Copeland is the bestselling author of the *Prayers That Avail Much*® family of books. The books are now in several languages, and there are more than three million copies in print.

She is the daughter of the late Reverend A. H. "Buck" and Donnis Brock Griffin. Germaine lives with her husband, Everette, in Roswell, Georgia. They have four children, ten grandchildren, and five great-grandchildren.

MISSION STATEMENT
Word Ministries, Inc.

To motivate individuals to spiritual growth
and emotional wholeness,
encouraging them to become more deeply
and intimately acquainted
with the Father God
as they pray prayers that avail much.

You may contact Word Ministries by writing
Word Ministries, Inc.
38 Sloan Street
Roswell, Georgia 30075
or calling 770-518-1065
www.prayers.org

*Please include your testimonies
and praise reports when you write.*

Other Books by Germaine Copeland

A Call to Prayer

The Road God Walks

Prayers That Avail Much Commemorative Gift Edition

Prayers That Avail Much Commemorative Leather Edition

Prayers That Avail Much for Business

Prayers That Avail Much Volume 1

Prayers That Avail Much Volume 1 — mass market edition

Prayers That Avail Much Volume 2

Prayers That Avail Much Volume 2 — mass market edition

Prayers That Avail Much Volume 3

Prayers That Avail Much Volume 3 — mass market edition

Prayers That Avail Much for Men

Prayer That Avail Much for Dads — pocket edition

Prayers That Avail Much for Women

Prayers That Avail Much for Women — pocket edition

Prayers That Avail Much for Mothers — hardbound

Prayers That Avail Much for Mothers — paperback

Prayers That Avail Much for Moms — pocket edition

Prayers That Avail Much for Teens — hardbound

Prayers That Avail Much for Teens — mass market edition

Prayers That Avail Much for Graduates — pocket edition

Prayers That Avail Much for Kids

Prayers That Avail Much for Kids — Book 2

Prayers That Avail Much for the Workplace

Oraciones Con Poder — *Prayers That Avail Much*
(Spanish Edition)

```
      4 10        1    ͛
  25.11      599
  11 95      599
 ─────────  ──────
 1 3 1 6 11.98

              3 4 9
              4 89
              ─────
  4.49         8.38        1.22 credit
 ═════                     .61 each


 11.98 ½   Prod          599
  4.49 ½   ship          224
  1.48 ½   +tax           74
                        ──────
                         8.97

   1 1 1                  8 38
  17.35                 ───────
   897                   17.35
 ───────                 ┌───────┐
  2 6.3 2                │ 16.74 │
                         └───────┘
                           8 38
```